Are you the living dead
or are you alive

© Little Book Publishing LLC
2023

So many people today truly believe they are living life and everything is right. They go about their day with a good routine and values. They believe hard work brings the most out of life. They consider themselves to be productive and have a good head on their shoulders. All good things none the less.

When we look on the surface there seems to be a rule book to each play, but let's look a little deeper for more awareness.
Begin to awaken yourself in a world that makes you become a dead man walking.

To start off, there isn't anything wrong with having a good routine and good values in life. Many people in the world have these great qualities. But, there is a difference with people that are living without awareness (dead) and those people that are truly alive (having awareness).

Let me give you an example of what I mean

when I say a dead person. First of all, they clearly have a pulse. When I say dead, I mean in the since of not knowing what the world truly has to offer. Their awareness level. Many times I have laid awake at night and can't sleep because there are so many things in the world that make me think about how I want to live differently. The thoughts remind me of how alive I am in the world. When you have so many things on your mind that it keeps you awake then the world is definitely keeping you busy. A lot of what keeps most people up at night is the fact that they are looking for change. You are up trying to find solutions to problems that affect your life during the day.

These problems then begin to consume you, so that in time your night stress becomes your day stress too. People then see this stress in your face. For others this may not be the case.

Some people seem to have life figured out and have become used to their 9 to 5 job and sex with their significant other every Wednesday. These people come to work faithfully and don't like to miss a day. This type of person lives a very robotic life. The routine is so routine that they could do this in their sleep. Dinner with his/her parents every other Sunday. Date night Saturday at 6pm in the usual place. Take the kids to practice on Tuesdays and Thursdays. etc. With each day being the same, there really isn't much of anything exciting to look forward to. These people typically try to find an outlet to help deal with the boring life structure. Some will begin to drink, or try to do things outside of the home, or even cheat just for the excitement. Others will fall into a depression.

Then we have the dreamer. They dream about all the things that they want to do but never do them. They tell everyone that they have big plans, but still, to this day, they are doing the same thing they were doing years ago.

Another group of people I like to call the complainers. These are people who complain a lot about the laws and rules of their state or even country. Or just about anything they feel is not fair. These people talk about who they believe should be in charge so laws and regulations can be changed. But if you have noticed these people never take action. They never go out to get anyone to sign a petition to change anything. They don't fight for the rights or freedom of society. These people can only speak on these situations and never have any real desire to be the one to establish the change that is actually needed.

What I am getting at is this is not living. The world has programed you into moving in one direction, but the world has many avenues.

When you get to a 4 way stop you have 3 other directions in which you can travel, yet you always seem to go

else's opinion or studies?
We as human beings all
contribute to this world;
so then why are so many
of us not living? Why
don't we have our own
beliefs of what this
world is all about?

So now you ask me.
What does it mean to
live, to be alive? Living is
everything. It is
laughing, crying,
loving, sharing, and
contributing. I am sure

you can find many words for being alive, so I gave just a few. To be alive means that you don't focus so much on what the world says is best, but you find out what is best for you. If you have a job that you've been at for a long time, make decent money, and it pays your bills, but it doesn't make you too eager to get out of bed then you are probably dead. You are contributing to a seat filler at a special event but you aren't really being noticed. Whether you showed up or not doesn't really make a difference to the company because they will still continue to be in business. Eventually, you will be replaced. If you had a job that meant something to you, then you would be more likely to be at work, or find a replacement if you can't make it in. We all make sacrifices for the things we really want. This can be in any aspect of your life. From relationships, to careers, or even religion. We enjoy working when it makes us happy and is rewarding.

I want to stop a minute and give you a simple exercise. Sometime throughout your week, I want you to just stop and observe the people around you. You can be at a coffee shop, work, home, or wherever. I am not wanting you to stare down anyone but watch them as best as you can. Imagine what their day might have been like. Does the person seem like they may have a routine? Are they happy? Does the person seem sidetracked easily? Even though you don't know the people you are watching there will be a pattern to them. When you are alive you can see the dead among you. Day in and day out you will see these people in a zombie like form.

A lot of times when you are dead you see what is in front of you as being normal. But what is normal? Everyone doing the same thing day in and day out with no feeling? Living requires change, inconsistencies, and feeling. If everyone is the same, then what are they contributing to the world? How can we tell one from another? Normal is that everyone is not the same, but that we all share the same creation. We are all humans who have different stories to tell and different views to share. We are to share space with others and teach each other. Share a moment to laugh or cry, learn or teach, work or relax but we do these things to complete this world.

I love to travel. It is just something that I love to do very much. I love to see new places and explore with new faces. This is something that I truly enjoy. Living doesn't mean you have to see the world; it means that you find meaning to your life, in this world. If you want to live, then do the things that you love as long as they contribute to happiness in the world. By this I simply mean if you are a serial killer then I don't suggest that you continue to kill because you enjoy it. The only way to live is knowing that your life has meaning and that your heart has feelings. All of the emotions that one can feel needs to be felt at different parts of your life. These feelings will build growth for you in your life. All of these feelings may not feel so good such as anger, disappointment, and regret, but without those moments you wouldn't be able to tell when you have the good moments. And if you have read my 1st book, then you know that I am one that lives in the moment. For the moment is all we have because after that is only the past.

Now is the time to make the world yours. Embrace your talents and knowledge and share them with one another. Now is the time to start treating others the way you would treat yourself. If you like root beer floats, then treat your friend to one. Don't get them the kiddie scoop. Lol

So how do we start making the change to be alive? In simplicity start living. Think about what you have been missing out on. Find the things that bring excitement or joy to your life. If you are a thrill seeker and haven't been able to climb that mountain, then make plans to do so. If you are like me and enjoy writing, then start. Get your paper and pen or computer out and start writing. If you enjoy helping others, then get involved in something where you can do that. All I am saying is don't wait for something in your life to happen on its own. If you do this, then nothing is ever going to happen because who or what are you waiting on? Is there supposed to be something fall out of the sky to make you get up out of your seat and get moving? Do you think there will be someone come into your life to wake you up? What are you waiting for? Give life a chance. Feel the freedom in changing your routine. Feel the freedom in changing how you make important decisions in your life. I promise you that you will feel so alive when you take a different path. When you see that the world gives you options and you start to take them, watch how life will become more enjoyable.

There is nothing more rewarding than saying to yourself I did it. I have removed the fear and started to live. I stopped hiding in the shadows and stepped out into the light. If people didn't see you before, trust me when I say they will see you now. Living in itself will bring people to notice you. But this is not about others. This is truly about self-awareness. If you are aware of things and how they affect you then you will be able to cope better or change how you go about things. I dare you to take a different path to get to work. I dare you to go into work and tell them the great ideas you have to better the company. Confidence comes with time but definitely with experience. If you never speak your mind, then you will never be heard. If you never tell anyone your great ideas, then how will they ever be heard. If you never explore new avenues, how will you know what is out there? We need everyone to contribute.

Find what it is that you are good at and use it to better this world. Get in a place to receive and accept change.

Writing for me is relaxing. I find this to be my comfort and my enjoyment because I believe that I have something to share with the world. I feel my writing will help people or maybe just reach one person. Either way I am doing what I enjoy.

I began writing when I was 14 but I didn't think it was going to be something I did as an adult. I began to write because I didn't have anyone to talk to. Writing made me feel as if I was out letting my problems to someone. Except, with writing I could go back and read how I was feeling and better understand myself. I could find solutions to my own problems just by reading what the problem was. I would feel better after I got things off my chest. It was my way of relieving stress. And believe it or not, I still use this method today. It has made me better understand myself and has helped me to connect with my feelings.

Change starts with you. If people, such as Martin Luther King Jr or Susan B Anthony can make a change then so can you.

Everyone will not do things in this world on a grand scale, but every event counts. Every event matters because no matter how big or small they might be, you have shared a moment with someone that may have just completely changed their lives. If one person enjoys your company, then smile for you are not alone in this world.

Quick list
People that are dead

1. Cause problems for others
2. Are not happy with themselves
3. Find things to bother people
4. Live a life of regrets

5. Are never satisfied
6. Break rules to get what they want
7. Think more about what should be done and not what could be done
8. Have a hard time with change
9. Cannot seem to find happiness
10. Spend more time trying to look as though they are pleasing others just to gain self-satisfaction

11. Don't know how to change their routine

I could continue on with this list, but I think you get the picture.

People who are living
1. Have an inner peace
2. Smile for no reason at all
3. Enjoy trying new things
4. Does things to break routine
5. Are happy with

themselves and want to share that happiness with others
6. Has a creative side
7. Enjoys helping others
8. Finds pleasure in the small things
9. Treats others the way they would treat themselves
10. Doesn't boast but is confident
11. Optimistic

I wrote the list last because this isn't the

best way to look at one's life. You may read the lists and say, I am not any of those things on the 1st list but I have some of the qualities in the 2nd list. How many people go to church every Sunday and get a lesson from the priest or pastor but still don't have a clear understanding about what they have been taught. Living means finding the answers to things in YOUR life. If your job runs you and you don't run it, then you are causing yourself unrest. If the relationship you have with others weighs heavy on you, then those probably aren't the people you should hang around. Living is a way of finding happiness without pain. Love is the opposite of hurt but most say that love is pain. But love is love

and pain is pain. Those 2 things should never be associated with one another because they are different. Or as we teach our children, those words are opposites. Up and down, left and right, these words cannot have the same meaning. And yet somehow pain and love are always placed together.
Start opening your eyes to the idea of change and trying new

things. Do not get stuck in a routine. Do not always accept what society has chosen you to be. Awaken yourself and live. Find the inner you. Define peace as peace, love as love and pain as pain. Then know the difference between each.

In conclusion, remember to take a moment in your day to close your eyes and relax. Reach inside yourself and feel the positive energy that is eager to explore and grow. Tell yourself that there are no limits to the possibilities you can have in your life. Find ways to open new doors and then feel free to explore those new places. Challenge yourself to come out of your shell and feel some of the heat from the sun's rays. Then enjoy it. Enjoy learning and feel good about yourself.

There is nothing wrong with growth and change. I know you can do this. Self-love is the start for your new beginning and a fresh new outlook to your life. Give in and embrace change because things will never stay the same forever. Change is a part of life and will always be an option to you. You cannot change others, but you can change yourself and that is something that should never be forgotten. As a Christian woman the belief is that we are all sinners and which sins will God forgive us for? Yet, God already knows we are sinners and does not look for us to one day become saints. What he does look for from us is that we have the desire to change. That we understand the possibilities from changing and the power that we gain from it.

If awakening yourself each morning means that you must give yourself a little pinch to remind you that you are alive, then do this. If you notice that you have become numb to the things and people around you then take a moment to stop and reflect. Something is causing you to feel that change is not possible or that making a change will not work. If all change was easy then life wouldn't be a bumpy road full of turns, and ups and downs, but if you never try then you will never know the outcome.

Find yourself, love yourself, and be yourself, for these things are truly what will make this world a better place.

Thanks again for reading and I hope this book will be an inspiration for many.

www.ingramcontent.com/pod-product-compliance
Lightning Source LLC
Chambersburg PA
CBHW071038080526
44587CB00015B/2673